TRIESTE

TRAVEL GUIDE 2024

Discover Trieste's hidden gems and
ancient wonders in 2024 edition

Jay Pittman

COPYRIGHT © 2023 BY JAY PITTMAN

TABLE OF CONTENTS

CHAPTER ONE: INTRODUCTION

CHAPTER TWO: GETTING STARTED

CHAPTER THREE: DISCOVERING THE CITY

CHAPTER FOUR: HIDDEN GEMS

CHAPTER FIVE: ANCIENT WONDERS

CHAPTER SIX: CULINARY DELIGHTS

CHAPTER SEVEN: OUTDOOR ADVENTURES

CHAPTER EIGHT: ENTERTAINMENT AND NIGHTLIFE

CHAPTER NINE: SHOPPING GUIDE

CHAPTER TEN: ACCOMMODATION OPTIONS

CHAPTER ELEVEN: PRACTICAL TIPS

CHAPTER TWELVE: CONCLUSION

CHAPTER ONE: INTRODUCTION

Welcome to Trieste

The fascinating city of Trieste, which is tucked away on Italy's northeastern coast, extends a warm welcome to those seeking a blend of breathtaking scenery, a rich cultural heritage, and historical significance. A tapestry of architectural wonders, delectable cuisine, and a cozy Mediterranean atmosphere welcome you as you arrive at this enchanted location, setting the scene for an amazing encounter.

At the meeting point of three distinct cultures—Croatian, Italian, and Slovenian—Trieste has a distinct character created by centuries of historical developments and cultural interactions. Every historical period, from the Romans to the Austro-Hungarians, has left its permanent imprint on the city, resulting in a fascinating fusion of customs, architectural forms, and culinary traditions that make Trieste a very unique destination.

What's New in 2024 Edition

1. Cultural Extravaganza: Celebrating Variety: The 2024 Trieste edition invites guests to an extended cultural festival that highlights the vibrant variety of the city. Discover a wide range of activities, such as international film festivals and art exhibits showcasing the abilities of regional and worldwide artists. Interact with the diverse array of cultures residing in Trieste.

2. Rejuvenated Waterfront: A Wander by the Ocean: Enjoy a leisurely walk along the recently renovated waterfront promenade, one of the city's highlights. Savor the allure of beachside cafés and craft stores while soaking in the stunning views of the Adriatic Sea. Nowadays, the waterfront acts as a center for leisure pursuits, offering a beautiful environment to both residents and visitors.

3. Cutting Edge Culinary Scene: Tasting Treats: In 2024, Trieste's restaurant scene will be the focus of attention thanks to an explosion of creative dining establishments and culinary adventures. Savor a gastronomic adventure that pushes the frontiers of innovation with classic Italian tastes combined with contemporary twists, prepared by famous chefs. Trieste has something to suit every taste, from elegant restaurants to quaint trattorias.

4. Tech Hub: Fostering Creative Thinking In 2024, Trieste, realizing its potential as a digital center, will debut innovative projects and startup incubators. Take advantage of tech conferences, seminars, and creatively collaborative places to interact with the city's vibrant innovation scene. In addition to being a historical treasure trove, Trieste is a progressive city influencing the future.

5. Green Projects: Trieste is Sustainable Trieste's dedication to sustainability is highlighted in the 2024 edition. Explore community-driven projects, green areas, and eco-friendly efforts that encourage environmental awareness. Trieste makes an effort to strike a balance between its allure from the past and its contemporary dedication to protecting the surrounding natural beauty.

6. Time Travel in Trieste for Immersive Historical Experiences Discover the rich history of the city by immersing yourself in various historical periods. Whether you want to stroll through medieval alleyways, explore Roman remains, or experience the splendor of the Habsburg period, Trieste beckons you to join in on its enthralling story.

7. Festivities & Events: An All-Year Extravaganza There are plenty of festivals and events scheduled for 2024 that appeal to a wide range of interests. There's always something going on in this vibrant city of Trieste, from music festivals that reverberate through old squares to cultural events that appreciate the city's marine heritage. To get the most out of your trip to Trieste, schedule your vacation around these occasions.

8. Hidden treasures Revealed: Off the Beaten Path Discover the best-kept secrets of Trieste with this carefully crafted guide to off-the-beaten-path hidden treasures. These hidden jewels provide a more personal and genuine experience with the city, whether it's a cozy café with expansive views or a quiet art museum featuring regional artists.

9. Interactive Digital Guides: Take Your Time Discovering With interactive digital guides that suit different interests and tastes, you can easily navigate

Trieste. These guides provide a customized experience, so you can explore the city at your own pace—whether you're an art fan, history buff, or foodie.

10. Warm Accommodations: Stay in Style: The 2024 edition offers a variety of warm lodging options to suit a variety of interests and preferences. Every tourist to Trieste is guaranteed a fashionable and pleasant stay, whether they want to stay in contemporary luxury accommodations or boutique hotels with a hint of ancient charm.

Finally, Trieste extends an invitation for you to join them on a trip through culture, history, and innovation in its 2024 edition. Its vibrant culinary scene, restored waterfront, and dedication to sustainability allow the city to harmoniously combine its historic past with a contemporary, vibrant attitude.

CHAPTER TWO: GETTING STARTED

Travelers are drawn to the little city of Trieste, which is tucked away on Italy's northeastern edge, by its breathtaking scenery, varied culture, and rich history. Traveling to Trieste offers a unique and unforgettable experience, regardless of your level of travel expertise. We'll cover all you need to know about travel and transportation in this guide to make sure your trip to Trieste is easy and pleasant.

Travel Essentials

1. Passport and Visa Requirements: Make sure your passport is valid for at least six months after the date of your intended departure before arriving in Trieste. Since Italy is a member of the Schengen Area, brief visits may require a Schengen visa, depending on your nationality. Verify the most recent admission standards and make sure you have the required paperwork well in advance.

2. Money and Banking: The Euro (EUR) is Italy's official currency. Being a part of Italy, Trieste has a robust financial infrastructure and is well served by ATMs. To ensure that using your credit or debit cards overseas won't cause any problems, let your bank know when you will be traveling. Keep extra cash on hand in case smaller businesses don't take credit or debit cards.

3. Language: Trieste's official language is Italian. Even though English is widely spoken in tourist locations, knowing a few simple Italian phrases can improve your stay and strengthen your bonds with the people. For easy access, have a phrasebook with you or utilize language applications.

4. Weather and Clothes: Trieste has pleasant winters and warm summers due to its

Mediterranean environment. Make sure you pack for the weather by checking the forecast for the dates of your trip. It's advised to wear light clothes, comfortable walking shoes, and a jacket for chilly nights. When traveling in the winter, pack layers of clothing and a water-resistant jacket.

5. Health and Safety: Although the healthcare system in Italy is dependable, it is still a good idea to obtain travel insurance that will pay for medical costs. Bring a basic first-aid kit and any prescription drugs that may be required. In general, Trieste is secure; nonetheless, use caution in busy places and keep your valuables away from pickpockets.

Transportation Tips

1. Getting to Trieste: Trieste-Friuli Venezia Giulia Airport (TRS) is the main entry point into Trieste. You may take a cab, shuttle bus, or rental vehicle from the airport to go to the city center. If you're traveling from a neighboring city, you could enjoy a beautiful ride on the train or bus.

2. Public Transportation: The bus and tram networks in Trieste are part of an effective public transportation system. Get your tickets on board or from kiosks, then verify them when you get on. Taxis are also widely accessible, although it's best to settle on a price before you go off.

3. Walking: The easiest way to see Trieste's small city center is on foot. Explore the area's ancient streets, stop at famous sites like Piazza Unità d'Italia, and take advantage of the café culture. Put on comfy shoes and take in the distinct vibe of the city.

4. Car Rentals: If you want to go to other nations or visit the scenic surrounding locations, you may want to think about hiring a car. There are several car-rental companies in Trieste, and having your own car gives you itinerary freedom. Become familiar with the parking and traffic laws in your area.

5. Day Trips and Beyond: Trieste is a great starting point for short excursions to neighboring sights. Drive down the Adriatic coast for a picturesque experience, or see the Miramare Castle with its stunning views. There are more exploring opportunities due to the close proximity to Slovenia and Croatia.

6. Cycling in Trieste: With designated bike lanes, Trieste is a bike-friendly city. have a bike rental and take a leisurely tour of the city. For a more difficult ride with breathtaking vistas, go to the adjacent Karst Plateau or cycle along the shoreline.

7. Boat Transportation: Trieste, a seaside city, provides boat services for an unforgettable view of the area. Think about taking a ferry to adjacent coastal towns or an Adriatic Sea boat excursion. Especially during the busiest travel seasons, confirm schedules and availability ahead of time.

8. Rail Travel: Given Italy's vast and well-functioning railway system, rail travel is a practical choice. Take a train ride via neighboring cities like Venice or Ljubljana for a relaxing and beautiful experience. If you want to save money, get your tickets in advance.

In summary

Beginning your journey in Trieste entails a smooth fusion of planning, discovery, and gratitude for the city's many resources. You can confidently traverse Trieste by being aware of crucial travel information and transit advice, which will guarantee that your time in this alluring Italian jewel is rewarding and unforgettable. So gather your belongings, immerse yourself in the culture, and watch as Trieste's magic happens before your eyes. Happy travels!

CHAPTER THREE: DISCOVERING THE CITY

Situated at the intersection of the Italian, Slovenian, and Croatian cultures, Trieste is a city with a thriving cultural scene, rich history, and many districts that are just waiting to be discovered. Let's explore the core of this fascinating city.

Historical Overview

The history of Trieste is a woven tapestry of Habsburg, Byzantine, Venetian, and Roman influences. The city was a mixing pot of cultures due to its advantageous position on the Adriatic Sea, and the rise and fall of regional dominance is reflected in its history.

Established in the second century BC as a Roman colony, Trieste prospered during the Byzantine Empire until succumbing to Venetian dominance in the fifteenth century. The magnificent Piazza Unità d'Italia is only one example of the city's architectural legacy that the Venetians left behind.

After assuming power, the Habsburgs turned Trieste into a significant port and center of commerce. During this time, the city's exquisite palaces and coffee shops were built, and they still stand today. The challenges of the 20th century included the redrawing of boundaries after World Wars I and II, which gave Trieste a distinct identity molded by its complicated past.

Cultural Highlights

Trieste's theaters, museums, and festivals all showcase the city's vibrant culture. The city is home to the Archaeological Museum, which explores its prehistoric history, and the Revoltella Museum, which showcases modern art. Readers who are interested in literature may visit the James Joyce Museum, which honors the well-known writer who lived a considerable amount of time in Trieste.

Cultural icons, the Teatro Verdi and the Teatro Romano, provide a wide range of shows. The scenic Gulf of Trieste attracts both sailors and spectators during its yearly Barcolana Regatta, which is one of the biggest sailing competitions globally. Trieste is also well-known for this event.

Neighborhood Exploration

Ancient Town (Vecchia Città)

Città Vecchia, the center of Trieste, is a maze of winding alleys, quaint squares, and old buildings. Situated on a hill, the San Giusto Cathedral provides expansive views of the city below. Explore the bustling Piazza Unità d'Italia, which is encircled by magnificent buildings like the Palazzo del Governo.

Teresiano Borgo

Borgo Teresiano, a landmark of Habsburg influence, is renowned for its neoclassical architecture. Wander along the elegantly designed Grand Canal and take in the energy of Piazza Ponterosso. Notable features include the Opicina Tramway, a historic funicular, and the Trieste Stock Exchange.

San Giusto

The San Giusto Castle perches atop San Giusto Hill, giving the city its crown. The castle and its environs provide a window into the medieval history of Trieste. Nature enthusiasts are welcome to take peaceful walks among luxuriant foliage in the Romanesque Revoltella Park.

Miramare

Visit the picturesque park and castle of Miramare for a peaceful getaway. The inside of the castle, which was constructed by Archduke Ferdinand

Maximilian, has sumptuous Habsburg furniture. The large gardens with their view of the Adriatic Sea provide a tranquil haven.

In summary, Trieste is a city that reveals facets of its past and present at every step. Every experience, whether it is seeing historic sites, immersing oneself in the arts, or strolling through interesting neighborhoods, adds a dimension to this captivating jewel of the Adriatic.

CHAPTER FOUR: HIDDEN GEMS

Adventuresome tourists are invited to explore Trieste, a fascinating city tucked away on Italy's northeastern coast. There are a ton of undiscovered treasures just waiting to be found. While well-known landmarks like Piazza Unità d'Italia and Miramare Castle attract large crowds, the city's true beauty may also be found in undiscovered areas and among local favorites.

Secret Spots Off the Beaten Path

1. Grotta Gigante: One of the biggest tourist caverns in the world is hidden under the surface of Trieste and is called Grotta Gigante. This enormous cavern has amazing stalactite formations and is a captivating subterranean realm. Visitors may explore its underground treasures with a guided tour, which offers a unique viewpoint on the geological history of the city.

2. Teatro Romano: The Roman Theatre is a historic treasure that is often missed by tourists. It is tucked away in the center of Trieste. This well-preserved amphitheater dates to the first century AD and was the site of gladiator fights and entertainment. It still serves as a serene haven from the busy streets and a reminder of Trieste's rich past.

3. Barcola Promenade: A charming length of the Adriatic Sea, the Barcola Promenade draws inhabitants looking for a calm getaway. Admire breathtaking views of the Gulf of Trieste and the Miramare Castle in the distance from this undiscovered beauty. It's the perfect place for a relaxed afternoon picnic or a leisurely walk.

4. Museo Revoltella Gardens: The Revoltella Gardens are a secret haven just next to the Revoltella Museum. With its fountains, sculptures, and colorful vegetation, this peaceful area offers the ideal escape from the bustle of the city. Because of its serene atmosphere, locals treasure this hidden paradise.

5. Città Vecchia: Although the Old Town isn't totally off the beaten track, its little lanes and secret courtyards are home to hidden gems. Discover the essence of Trieste by exploring the Città Vecchia, which is home to quaint cafés, artisan stores, and old buildings.

Local Favorites

1. Osmiza: Go to an Osmiza to really immerse yourself in the regional cuisine. These are family-run businesses that sell cheeses, cured meats, and wines prepared in-house. Locals visit these hidden jewels often because they provide a true sense of Trieste's culinary history.

2. Buffet do Pepi: A well-liked local institution, Buffet da Pepi offers a taste of authentic Triestine food. For more than a century, this iconic restaurant has been offering traditional fare, including jota, or bean and sauerkraut soup, and a variety of marine delicacies.

3. Caffè degli Specchi: Although Piazza Unità d'Italia is a popular destination, well-informed residents frequent Caffè degli Specchi. This old-world charm is evident in this ancient bistro that is filled with mirrors and antique furnishings. Enjoy an aperitivo or coffee while taking in the sophisticated atmosphere.

4. Rilke Trail: Head a few ways outside the city limits to the Rilke Trail, a picturesque seaside promenade bearing the poet Rainer Maria Rilke's name. This beloved spot among the locals provides amazing views of the sea and the rocks. It's a well-liked location for Triestini to take a reflective stroll.

5. Pasticceria Penso: A beloved pastry store among the locals, indulge your sweet craving at Pasticceria Penso. Dessert aficionados will find nirvana in this hidden treasure, which offers inventive delicacies as well as classic pastries like putizza.

In summary

Trieste's many facets are enhanced by its hidden treasures, which may be found both off the usual route and among the city's favorites. Discover the real spirit of Trieste beyond its famous sites by venturing into subterranean caverns, enjoying regional food, or meandering through secret gardens.

CHAPTER FIVE: ANCIENT WONDERS

Rich in cultural diversity and history, Trieste is a city known for its architectural wonders and ancient wonders that highlight its historical importance. Let's explore the historical sites and architectural treasures that make Trieste a veritable gold mine of antiquated masterpieces.

Historical Landmarks

1. Trieste's Roman Theatre: Constructed in the first century AD, the Roman Theatre is a reminder of Trieste's Roman history. Situated in the center of the city, it used to hold thousands of people who came to see different shows. The remarkably intact remnants provide an insight into the Roman Empire's architectural capabilities.

2. Trieste Cathedral (Cattedrale di San Giusto): Perched atop San Giusto Hill, overlooking the city, the cathedral is a testament to the religious and historical importance of the area. Built in the sixth century, it experienced a number of reconstructions that combined Gothic and Romanesque architectural elements. The cathedral has sweeping views over Trieste and is home to priceless artwork.

3. Castle of Miramare: The 19th-century architectural masterpiece, the Castle of Miramare, was commissioned by Austria's Archduke Ferdinand Maximilian. The castle, which is perched on the Gulf of Trieste, blends Neoclassical and Romantic architectural features. It is a historical monument that is a must-see because of its magnificent grounds and expansive vistas.

4. Arco di Riccardo, also known as the Arch of Richard: This historic Roman gate serves as a portal to Trieste's history. As an honor to Emperor Augustus, this triumphal arch is said to have been built in the first century. History buffs will find it to be an engrossing sight because of its minute intricacies and historical relevance.

5. Piazza Unità d'Italia: One of the biggest squares in Europe and a center of historical importance is Piazza Unità d'Italia, the main plaza of Trieste. The plaza, which is surrounded by imposing structures like the Town Hall and the Government Palace, has been the site of important historical occasions and is a popular destination for both residents and visitors.

Archaeological Marvels

1. Aquileia Archaeological Area: Located close to Aquileia, although not quite in Trieste, this area is rich in Roman ruins. It is a UNESCO World Heritage Site with elaborate mosaics, a forum, and old Roman roadways. Trieste's historical charm is enhanced by Aquileia's close vicinity.

2. Roman Walls: The ruins of the city's walls encircle Trieste and provide insight into its former defenses. Constructed for defensive reasons, these walls emphasize Trieste's strategic significance across the ages.

3. Muggia Archaeological Park: Set in the picturesque village of Muggia, close to Trieste, this archaeological park reveals centuries' worth of history. Discoveries of Roman villas, early Christian basilicas, and medieval buildings shed light on the many cultures that had inhabited the area.

4. San Rocco Castle: Situated on the Karst Plateau, this castle reveals artifacts that date back many centuries. The castle functions as a living museum, enabling visitors to examine the historical development of the Trieste area, showcasing everything from ancient items to medieval architecture.

5. The Prehistoric Cave of Trebiciano: The Prehistoric Cave of Trebiciano is a fascinating trip into the distant past for people who are interested in prehistory. The discovery of Neolithic and Bronze Age towns during excavations has provided insight into the prehistory of the Trieste region.

In summary, Trieste's historic treasures, which include everything from prehistoric caves and archaeological parks to Roman theaters and churches, form a mosaic of cultural and historical value. In addition to serving as reminders of the city's history, these wonders and monuments entice tourists to go on an enthralling voyage through time. Trieste's tenacity and continuing allure are shown by the way it has managed to integrate its antique riches with the contemporary environment.

CHAPTER SIX: CULINARY DELIGHTS

The northeastern Italian port city of Trieste is a fascinating place with a rich culinary legacy shaped by its unique history and physical location. We'll dive into the regional cuisine on this tour of Trieste's culinary pleasures, emphasizing its distinctive tastes and customs. We'll also provide restaurant suggestions for a fully immersive culinary adventure in this charming city.

Local Cuisine

1. Historical context and influencing factors

Because of its lengthy history as a significant port city, Trieste's culinary culture is a melting pot of influences. It has been ruled by the Italian state, the Venetian Republic, and the Austro-Hungarian Empire throughout the years. The local cuisine has been permanently impacted by this blending of cultures.

2. Recipes You Must Try

a. Jota: A traditional Trieste soup, Jota is prepared with sauerkraut, beans, potatoes, and smoked pig. This meal is the epitome of Slavic and Italian culinary fusion.

b. Fish Fritto Misto

Trieste is well known for its seafood because of its seaside setting. A dish of gently fried mixed fish called fritto misto di pesce highlights the abundance of fresh seafood found in the Adriatic.

c. Busara Escargot

With Scampi alla Busara, a dish of langoustines cooked in a flavorful tomato and wine sauce, Trieste's love affair with shellfish continues.

d. The Triestino Goulash

Goulash Triestino is a regional take on the traditional Hungarian goulash, evoking memories of the city's Austro-Hungarian heritage. Usually, it consists of delicate beef cooked with potatoes, onions, and paprika.

e. The Jota of Trieste

A classic dessert, La Jota Triestina, is not to be confused with the soup Jota. It's a pastry loaded with honey, almonds, and spices that symbolizes the sweet side of Trieste's cuisine.

3. The Culture of Coffee

Because of its long history with the coffee trade, Trieste has a strong coffee culture. Enjoy an espresso at one of the city's iconic coffee shops, such as Caffè San Marco or Caffè degli Specchi, where the craft of brewing coffee is celebrated as an artistic endeavor.

Dining Recommendations

1. Conventional Osterie

a. Da Marino Osteria

Osteria da Marino is a classic Triestine osteria, tucked away in the center of the ancient town. It has a warm atmosphere and a cuisine full of regional specialties. Their Fritto Misto di Pesce and Jota are not to be missed.

b. Panada Antico

The place to go if you want a flavor of Austro-Hungarian heritage is Antico Panada. This restaurant's Goulash Triestino is a gastronomic marvel, and the atmosphere takes guests back in time.

2. The Excellence of Seafood

a. Giovanni's Tavern

Trattoria da Giovanni, well-known for its Scampi alla Busara, is a seafood lover's dream come true. A selection of freshly caught seafood cooked with a hint of Trieste's culinary flare is included on the menu.

b. La Pescheria

La Pescheria, which is close to the fish market, provides a distinctive eating experience. The chefs will expertly cook any seafood that guests pick from the market to perfection.

3. Culinary Investigation

a. Eataly Trieste

Eataly Trieste is a refuge for those seeking a more extensive gastronomic experience. The best regional goods are gathered at this Italian marketplace, giving guests the chance to discover and sample the wide range of regional delicacies.

b. Food Tour of Trieste

Take a guided culinary tour to discover the mysteries of Trieste's cuisine. Visitors are often led by local guides through classic restaurants, marketplaces, and coffee shops, offering them insights into the culinary history of the city.

In summary

Trieste's rich history and diverse culture are reflected in its gastronomic offerings. The city's cuisine is a feast for the senses, with everything from flavorful soups to succulent seafood. Through the exploration of traditional osterie, the joys of seafood, and culinary excursions, travelers may fully immerse themselves in the distinct and rich world of Trieste's culinary delights.

CHAPTER SEVEN: OUTDOOR ADVENTURES

Nestled on Italy's northeastern coast, the city of Trieste skillfully combines culture, history, and scenic beauty. The area is well-known for its magnificent architecture and rich maritime history, but it is also a refuge for outdoor enthusiasts and nature lovers due to its abundance of outdoor activities. We shall explore the wide range of outdoor adventures and wilderness getaways that Trieste has to offer in this in-depth guide.

Nature Escapes

1. Karst Plateau: A Wonder of Geology

Encircling Trieste lies the natural marvel known as the Karst Plateau, which stretches over the border between Slovenia and Italy. The plateau, which is well-known for its unusual limestone formations, presents a bizarre terrain filled with sinkholes, caverns, and subterranean rivers. The Kocjan Caves, a UNESCO World Heritage Site, are a must-see location where tourists may explore expansive caverns and see firsthand how the Reka River chisels through the limestone.

2. Grotta Gigante: A Massive Subterranean Universe

Grotta Gigante is a must-visit location for everyone looking for an underground experience. Impressive stalactites and stalagmites decorate this enormous cave, which is among the biggest in the world. Guided tours show guests the secret geological history and lead them through rooms with astonishing acoustics.

3. Val Rosandra: An Organic Sanctuary

Val Rosandra provides a revitalizing getaway into nature and is just a short drive from Trieste. Hiking and trekking enthusiasts will find a gorgeous environment as the Rosandra River crisscrosses this verdant valley. For those who like the outdoors, the trails' winding paths through woods, past waterfalls, and sweeping overlooks make for the ideal day trip.

4. Miramare Park: A serene coastal area

Despite the fact that Trieste is a seaside city, Miramare Park is a particularly tranquil coastal retreat. The Miramare Castle is surrounded by a park with breath-taking views of the Adriatic Sea. The old castle, lovely gardens, and waterfront picnics provide the perfect combination of history and natural beauty for visitors.

Recreational Activities

1. Sailing Adventures: Navigating the Adriatic Sailing possibilities in Trieste bring the city's maritime legacy to life. Sailors love the Gulf of Trieste because of its consistent breezes. Both inexperienced and seasoned sailors may take advantage of sailing trips, which let them explore the coastline, take in expansive city vistas, and even take part in regattas on special occasions.

2. Hiking Trails: Take a Foot Exploration of the Karst Landscape

Because of its varied terrain, the Karst Plateau has a vast network of hiking paths. These paths lead to secret caverns, expansive views, and charming towns. They range in difficulty from family-friendly strolls to strenuous treks for experienced hikers. The Rilke Trail, named after the well-known poet Rainer Maria Rilke, is a very picturesque path that winds around the Karst cliffs.

3. Cycling Paths: Travel Through Stunning Sceneries

Trieste is a cyclist's paradise, offering a range of riding routes suitable for all levels of ability. A disused railroad-converted bike route, the Parenzana Trail passes through quaint towns, olive orchards, and vineyards. On two wheels, cyclists may enjoy the freedom of exploring the region's varied landscapes.

4. Carso Rock Climbing: Vertical Experiences

Rock climbers will find great fun in the rugged terrain of the Carso, the limestone plateau that encircles Trieste. The cliffs and crags provide climbing lovers with vertical difficulties that may be tackled on routes that suit different ability levels. Regional guides help more experienced climbers find undiscovered treasures in the area and aid novices.

In summary

For outdoor aficionados, Trieste is a paradise because of its unique combination of natural beauty and leisure activities. Experiences abound in the city and its environs, whether venturing into the enigmatic depths of the Karst Plateau, sailing the Adriatic, or going on an adventurous bicycle ride.

Trieste's dedication to protecting its natural assets guarantees that tourists may enjoy outdoor experiences while taking in the splendor of this exceptional Italian city.

CHAPTER EIGHT: ENTERTAINMENT AND NIGHTLIFE

Nestled on the northeastern coast of Italy, Trieste is a city renowned for its lively entertainment and nightlife scene, in addition to its rich history and breathtaking architecture. Both residents and tourists may choose from a wide variety of alternatives in Trieste, from theaters featuring compelling performances to vibrant nightlife locations.

Theatres and Performances

Romano Theater

Located on San Giusto Hill's slopes, Teatro Romano is one of Trieste's most well-known theaters. This first-century AD Roman theater offers a distinctive backdrop for a variety of acts. It can hold around 3,500 people for plays, concerts, and dance events, among other traditional and modern works.

Teatro Giuseppe Verdi Lirico

The Teatro Lirico Giuseppe Verdi is a tribute to Trieste's cultural legacy for visitors looking for a more conventional theatrical experience. This opera theater, named after the well-known Italian composer, has a 19th-century past. It still hosts classical music, ballet, and opera events, drawing both local and foreign performers.

Rossetti Politeama

Another legendary location in Trieste's performing arts landscape is Politeama Rossetti. Originally built in the late 1800s, this theater has undergone many modifications to preserve its opulence. It can host a range of events, including musical concerts and theatrical plays. There is something for every taste thanks to the varied programming, which appeals to both residents and visitors.

Modern Performances

Trieste is not only about traditional art; it also welcomes modern performers. Modern music concerts, avant-garde dance performances, and experimental theater are held at various locations across the city, including Cavana Quarter. These shows, which often target a younger audience, add to the vibrant cultural environment of the city.

Nightlife Hotspots

Italy's Unità Piazza

Piazza Unità d'Italia, Trieste's central plaza, is a center of nightlife in addition to being a historical and architectural treasure. The area, surrounded by tasteful buildings and brightened by quaint lamps, comes to life at night. Many cafés and bars provide the ideal setting for a restful evening, making it a well-liked gathering spot for both residents and visitors.

Caffe degli Specchi

The classic and ageless Caffè degli Specchi is located in Piazza Unità d'Italia. It has been open since the 19th century and offers a classy atmosphere for an evening drink. With outside seating, customers can take in the vibrant vibe of the area while enjoying a refreshing beverage or a traditional Italian espresso.

Le Rive

Le Rive, a group of eateries and pubs along the Canal Grande, is a good option for people who would rather be near the water. When the lights reflect on the river in the evening, providing a charming and romantic background, this place becomes even more magical. Take a leisurely walk along the canal or stop at one of the locations for a delicious lunch and refreshments.

Molo Audace

As the sun sets, the city's famous pier, Molo Audace, comes alive with activity. It provides a breathtaking view of the coastline and the Adriatic Sea. There are several pubs and clubs along the pier that provide a variety of entertainment alternatives, including DJ sets and live music. The sound of the waves and the sea wind enhance the special sensation of taking in Trieste's nightlife.

Clubs and bars in Old Town

There are many different pubs and clubs in Trieste's Old Town, which has small alleyways and old buildings. You may discover a venue that fits your tastes, whether they are in the form of jazz, electronic music, or just a nice, friendly pub. Old Town's vibrant vitality makes sure that nighttime doesn't only happen at certain places; it creates a lively, unplanned environment.

In summary

Trieste provides a varied entertainment and nightlife experience with its unique combination of historical charm and modern vitality. The city's dedication to cultural diversity is shown by the theaters, which range from classical opera houses to ancient Roman buildings. Whether you're looking for a quiet evening in a historic café or a vibrant night on the waterfront or in the heart of Old Town, the many nightlife locations appeal to a variety of interests. Residents and tourists alike are encouraged to immerse themselves in the lively cultural tapestry of Trieste via the entertainment and nightlife scene, which is distinguished by its diversity and inclusion.

CHAPTER NINE: SHOPPING GUIDE

The fascinating city of Trieste, which is located on Italy's northeastern coast, provides both residents and tourists with an enjoyable shopping experience. The retail scene in Trieste showcases the city's rich cultural legacy and many influences, offering everything from distinctive souvenirs to lively markets and quaint shops. With its emphasis on distinctive souvenirs and an exploration of the lively markets and shops that make Trieste a shopper's paradise, this in-depth shopping guide will take you on a tour through all the many aspects of shopping in the city.

Unique Souvenirs

Trieste offers a vast selection of distinctive mementos that encapsulate the spirit of the city's past and present. Whether you're searching for modern or traditional crafts, you're sure to discover something unique to bring home as a keepsake of your trip to Trieste.

Located in the core of the historic district, Bazzarre Triestine is a veritable gold mine of trinkets that are typical of Trieste. This area displays the creative legacy of the city with its well-created pottery, hand-painted masks, and exquisite lacework.

2. Antique bookshops: Known for their literary heritage, antique bookshops in Trieste, such as Libreria Antiquaria Umberto Saba, provide a distinctive assortment of rare books, old postcards, and literary artifacts. For book lovers, they are unique and thoughtful mementos.

3. Coffee-related Items: Trieste, a city with a strong coffee culture, has a wide selection of souvenirs linked to coffee. Seek out specialty coffee mixes that capture the essence of Trieste's caffeine-infused heritage, locally roasted coffee beans, and handcrafted coffee mugs.

4. A maritime motif Keepsakes: Because of Trieste's maritime past, there are many interesting sea-themed mementos available. Popular options include seashell décor, jewelry with a marine theme, and ship models.

5. Artwork with a Trieste theme: Look for one-of-a-kind paintings, prints, or sculptures that highlight Trieste's allure and beauty in nearby art studios and galleries. In their creations, local artists often depict the distinctive architecture and landscapes of the city.

Marketplaces and Boutiques

The markets and shops in Trieste provide a wide range of shopping options, from high-end couture to fresh fruit and regional crafts. By exploring these lively areas, you may fully experience the dynamic spirit of the city.

1. Piazza Unità d'Italia: Piazza Unità d'Italia, Trieste's major plaza, is the site of several outdoor markets and gatherings. This area is a hive of activity, with artisan fairs displaying handcrafted goods and lively markets offering fresh fruit and regional specialties.

2. Molo Audace Market: This quaint market, which is situated along the waterfront, is where locals sell their wares while taking in views of the Adriatic Sea. Fresh seafood, locally crafted crafts, and delicacies are all available here.

3. Boutique Shopping on Via San Nicolò: Via San Nicolò is the place to go if you're looking for upmarket retailers. Numerous chic stores along this street provide designer items, accessories, and couture clothing.

4. Old Stock Exchange Building: Formerly known as Palazzo della Borsa, the Old Stock Exchange Building is now a retail mall. Discover a variety of handmade stores, boutiques, and cafés nestled within the ancient surroundings of the building as you meander through its hallways.

5. Boutique vineyards: Trieste offers the chance to visit boutique vineyards because of its closeness to well-known wine areas. You may taste and buy great local wines in the city's tasting rooms and wine stores, which make for a wonderful memento.

To sum up, Trieste's retail scene offers a lively marketplace experience, a wide variety of souvenirs, and a beautiful fusion of heritage and modernity.

CHAPTER TEN: ACCOMMODATION OPTIONS

The northeastern Italian city of Trieste is a wonderful place to stay that can accommodate a range of tastes and price points. Travelers on a tight budget, luxury travelers, or those looking for a more intimate and customized experience can all find something to like in Trieste. We will examine the many lodging choices in Trieste in this thorough guide, including hotels, bed and breakfasts, and Airbnb suggestions.

Hotels

Trieste is home to a variety of hotels, ranging from lavish properties with expansive views of the sea to more affordable but cozy choices. Here are a few notable options at different pricing points:

1. Excelsior Palace in Savoia

The five-star Savoia Excelsior Palace is located on the seafront and is renowned for its opulent facilities and first-rate service. In addition to enjoying the hotel's restaurant and spa services, the accommodations have breathtaking views of the Gulf of Trieste.

2. Savoia Excelsior Palace Starhotels

Situated in the center of the city, this four-star hotel seamlessly blends sophistication with contemporary amenities. Major sights like Castello di Miramare and Piazza dell'Unità d'Italia are easily accessible on foot from the property. The hotel has a chic bar, a fitness facility, and roomy accommodations.

3. Hotel Trieste

The modern hotel NH Trieste is well situated close to the city center and train station. It's a well-liked option for both business and leisure tourists because of its stylish design, cozy accommodations, and rooftop patio.

4. Continental Hotel

The Hotel Continentale offers a convenient location and decent accommodations for guests looking for a mid-range choice. The hotel provides tidy, well-furnished rooms, and before seeing the city, visitors may savor a breakfast buffet.

5. Ghega Affittacamere

Affittacamere Ghega is a guesthouse that provides reasonably priced lodging without sacrificing comfort or cleanliness if you're on a tight budget. For visitors using public transit, its proximity to the train station is helpful.

Bed and Breakfast

A popular option for those seeking a more customized and intimate stay are bed and breakfasts, or B&Bs. There are a number of quaint

B&Bs in Trieste that provide a cozy setting and local knowledge.

1. Cassio B&B

B&B Cassio, housed in a historic structure, provides comfortable accommodations with a blend of contemporary and old furnishings. In addition to receiving a warm greeting from the welcoming hosts, visitors may enjoy a prepared breakfast that includes regional delicacies.

2. Julia of B&B Gens

B&B Gens Julia, which is in the heart of the city, is renowned for its cozy accommodations and kind hosts. The B&B is a great option for wandering around Trieste since it's close to all the major sites.

3. The Inn at Porta Cavana

B&B Porta Cavana is close to the waterfront and has quaint rooms with views of the sea for a beachside experience. Known for their warm hospitality, the hosts serve up a delicious breakfast for visitors to enjoy on the patio.

4. Trieste Plus B&B

The chic and contemporary lodging of B&B Trieste Plus is located right in the center of the city. For those searching for a cozy haven away from home, this B&B provides individualized attention to detail and a cozy refuge.

5. Fiori B&B

Familiar and genuine, B&B Fiori is a family-run business tucked away in a peaceful area. Visitors like the personal touch, and the B&B's convenient access to public transit makes it simple to explore the city.

Airbnb Recommendations

Airbnb provides a variety of distinctive lodging options in Trieste for people who would rather have a more autonomous and local experience. The following suggestions are provided:

1. Old Town Historic Apartment

With its lovely architecture and contemporary conveniences, this conveniently placed Airbnb property offers a look into Trieste's past. The ease of visiting neighboring eateries, cafés, and sites is available to guests.

2. Villa by the Sea with sweeping views

Think about hiring a coastal house with expansive views of the Adriatic Sea if you want a more private experience. This Airbnb choice puts you close to Trieste's attractions but still provides a peaceful haven.

3. A Contemporary Loft in an Artistic Neighborhood

Spend your time in a stylish neighborhood's artsy loft to fully immerse yourself in Trieste's thriving cultural scene. Walkable distances from this Airbnb include vibrant cafés, galleries, and stores.

Comfortable Studio Close to Miramare Castle

A comfortable apartment close to Miramare Castle might be a great option if you'd rather stay in a more sedate area close to the outdoors. This Airbnb offering offers a cozy location for unwinding and discovering the neighboring coastal regions.

5. Garden-Vented, Family-Friendly Apartment

Are you going on a family vacation? Take into consideration an Airbnb accommodation with a garden, which offers kids a fun and secure environment. This welcoming choice is perfect for families, as it provides a cozy ambiance and all the conveniences needed for a pleasant stay.

In conclusion, Trieste offers a wide variety of lodging choices to suit the needs of a wide spectrum of tourists. A stay at one of the city's elegant hotels, a quaint bed and breakfast, or an autonomous Airbnb stay will undoubtedly make your trip unforgettable. The city offers a distinctive fusion of natural beauty, history, and culture.

CHAPTER ELEVEN: PRACTICAL TIPS

Beautiful Trieste, located on Italy's northeast coast, combines breathtaking scenery, a diverse range of cultures, and a long history. To guarantee a seamless and pleasurable journey, it's important to put safety first and have access to helpful contacts while exploring this enchanted location.

Safety Information

1. General Advice on Safety

Although Trieste is generally considered secure, like with any city, it is important to exercise caution, particularly in congested areas and popular tourist destinations.

Pickpockets should be avoided, especially in crowded marketplaces, on public transit, and at tourist destinations.

Keep your possessions safe, and think about carrying a neck bag or money belt for valuables.

Pay attention to your surroundings, particularly while taking walks at night or in places with less traffic.

2. Medical and Health Facilities

The Italian healthcare system is excellent. In an emergency, contact 112 to get help right away.

Get acquainted with the locations of pharmacies and hospitals. Ospedale di Cattinara is Trieste's primary hospital.

Make sure your travel insurance includes hospitalization and emergency medical coverage.

3. Safety of Transportation

Trieste has a well-established bus and rail network for public transit. Take care of your possessions while traveling via public transportation.

In general, taxis are safe, although it's best to utilize authorized taxi stands or reliable ride-sharing applications.

Know the parking and traffic laws in the area if you want to hire a vehicle.

4. Meteorological Measures

Trieste has scorching summers and mild winters due to its Mediterranean environment. Keep yourself hydrated in the summer and prepare appropriately for the winter. Examine the weather, particularly if you want to visit outdoor sites or partake in outdoor activities like hiking.

5. Sensitivity to Culture

Being polite is valued among Italians. Acquire a few simple Italian words, since people there often value visitors who try to connect with them in their own tongue.

When attending places of worship, dress modestly and observe regional traditions and customs.

Useful Contacts

1. Emergency Assistance

Police: In non-emergency circumstances, dial 113 to request police help.

Medical Emergency: Press 112 to summon an ambulance or 112 for emergency medical help.

2. Consulates and embassies

Find out the address and phone number of the embassy or consulate of your nation in Trieste in case you need help with an emergency or passport-related matters.

3. Information Centers for Travelers

Maps, guidance, and useful information are available to travelers at the Tourist Information Office in Piazza Unità d'Italia.

4. Municipal Governments

City Hall: Get in touch with the neighborhood city hall with questions about non-emergency matters.

5. Contacts for Transportation

Trieste Airport: Get in touch with the information desk at Trieste Airport with questions about flights.

Train and Bus Stations: Keep your contact information handy for help or timetable information at the major train and bus stations.

6. Contacts at the Embassy or Consulate

Keep the contact details for the embassy or consulate of your nation on hand in case of an emergency, misplaced paperwork, or needing assistance from the consulate.

In summary

When traveling to Trieste, it's important to make sure you're secure and have access to the people you need. You can fully enjoy this fascinating city and its rich cultural offerings while maintaining your safety by being aware and adopting the appropriate safety measures.

CHAPTER TWELVE: CONCLUSION

The fascinating city of Trieste, which is tucked away on Italy's northeastern coast, is a unique tourist destination because of its varied culture, rich history, and breathtaking scenery. There are important things to think about when your trip comes to an end in Trieste, from summarizing your experience to organizing your future vacation. We will examine the importance of the finish in Trieste in depth in this comprehensive analysis, including details on the city's allure, notable sites, regional food, and useful advice for future trips.

Final Thoughts

Every visitor is left with a lasting impression of Trieste's unique combination of cosmopolitan energy and historical grandeur. The city's distinct identity is influenced by its complicated history as a component of many empires and its historical importance as a major port. When you wrap up your tour of Trieste, consider the marvels of architecture that line its streets.

Marvels of Architecture:

Trieste's many cultural influences may be seen in the city's unusual blend of architectural styles. Situated on a hill, the Cathedral of San Giusto provides expansive views of both the Adriatic Sea and the city. Visitors are enthralled by its Romanesque-Gothic architecture and elaborate mosaics, which provide an insight into the city's ecclesiastical past.

One of the biggest beachfront squares in Europe, Piazza Unità d'Italia, is a reminder of Trieste's imperial heritage. The area, which is surrounded by imposing structures like the Lloyd Triestino Palace and City Hall, is a center of activity that hosts events and meetings all year.

Literary and Cultural Legacies:

Poets and authors have traditionally looked to Trieste as inspiration. The city served as a source of inspiration for the well-known Irish writer James Joyce, whose writings you might examine. A trip to the James Joyce Museum offers a more profound understanding of the author's and Trieste's literary relationship.

The city's ongoing cultural legacy is on display at the old Roman amphitheater known as the Teatro Romano. It now functions as a location for events that combine the traditional with the modern.

Gourmet Treats: An Entire Gastronomic Exploration

Without indulging in Trieste's delectable cuisine, no visit is complete. The food of the city incorporates elements from Austrian, Italian, and Slovenian cuisines, reflecting its varied heritage. As you wrap up your gastronomic journey, take note of these highlights.

Culture of Coffee:

It is essential to pay a visit to one of Trieste's iconic cafés, which are well-known for their coffee culture. For more than a century, philosophers and artists have gathered at Caffè San Marco, which has a charming old-world feel about it. Savor a thick espresso cup and take in the ambience that has motivated many generations.

Superb Seafood Buffet:

Trieste, a city on the sea, has a wide variety of meals made with fresh fish. The famous Scampi alla Busara (langoustines in a tomato and wine sauce) and Boreto alla Triestina (fish stew) are just two examples of the delicious seafood dishes that the area has to offer.

Carso Wines:

To sample excellent wines, go to the Carso wine area, which is situated outside of Trieste. The specific terroir gives the local varietals, such as Terrano and Vitovska, their distinct qualities. See the enthusiasm of the vintners and enjoy the results of their effort by visiting a nearby vineyard.

Planning Your Next Adventure

Even when you say goodbye to Trieste, the memories you made here will be with you. In order to guarantee that your next travel experiences are just as rewarding, take into account these useful suggestions while organizing your itinerary.

Examining Adjacent Places:

Because of its advantageous position, Trieste is a great place to begin visiting nearby attractions. Head south to visit the medieval city of Pula in Croatia, or cross into Slovenia to experience the beauty of Ljubljana. There are many possibilities for your next journey due to the variety of landscapes and cultures that are near Trieste.

Seasonality to Consider:

The weather in Trieste is Mediterranean, with pleasant summers and moderate winters. When planning your next trip, take into account the season, since every season has its own special allure for the city. Fall and spring are especially nice seasons for exploring outdoor sites in comfort.

Immersion-Based Language Instruction:

Although the majority of people in Trieste speak Italian, there is also a sizable Slovenian-speaking community due to the city's closeness to Slovenia. To improve your communication skills with the locals, think about picking up some basic Slovenian and Italian vocabulary. Apps and internet resources for language study may be quite helpful in getting ready for a multilingual trip.

Concluding Remarks: An Entire Memoir

You bring a tapestry of memories from the history, culture, and cuisine of Trieste with you as your voyage comes to an end. Trieste's warmth and the legends woven into its alleys are just as captivating as its stunning architecture and mouthwatering food. Trieste extends an invitation to you to embrace its own essence, whether you seek comfort in the shady nooks of its antique cafés or are awestruck by the magnificence of its squares.

Allow your time in Trieste to act as a compass for your future travel plans, pointing you in the direction of places where history and culture are most beautifully shown. Your stay in Trieste is coming to a close, but your tour is far from over; there are still more places to discover. With its ageless appeal, Trieste says goodbye and opens the way for further exploration and experiences.

Printed in Great Britain
by Amazon

44145257R00046